INSIDE PROFESSIONAL SOCCER

FC BARCELONA

Heather Williams

MEDIA ENHANCED BOOKS
AV2 BY WEIGL
ADDED VALUE • AUDIO VISUAL
www.av2books.com

Go to **www.av2books.com**, and enter this book's unique code.

BOOK CODE

AVN35965

AV² by Weigl brings you media enhanced books that support active learning.

AV² provides enriched content that supplements and complements this book. Weigl's AV² books strive to create inspired learning and engage young minds in a total learning experience.

Your AV² Media Enhanced books come alive with...

Audio
Listen to sections of the book read aloud.

Video
Watch informative video clips.

Embedded Weblinks
Gain additional information for research.

Try This!
Complete activities and hands-on experiments.

Key Words
Study vocabulary, and complete a matching word activity.

Quizzes
Test your knowledge.

Slide Show
View images and captions, and prepare a presentation.

... and much, much more!

Published by AV² by Weigl
350 5th Avenue, 59th Floor
New York, NY 10118
Website: www.av2books.com

Library of Congress Control Number: 2018930407

ISBN 978-1-4896-7775-4 (hardcover)
ISBN 978-1-4896-7776-1 (softcover)
ISBN 978-1-4896-7777-8 (multi-user eBook)

Printed in the United States of America in Brainerd, Minnesota
1 2 3 4 5 6 7 8 9 0 22 21 20 19 18

022018
120817

Project Coordinator: John Willis   Designer: Terry Paulhus

The publisher acknowledges Getty Images, Alamy, Newscom, and Wikimedia as its primary image suppliers for this title.

INSIDE PROFESSIONAL SOCCER

CONTENTS

Introduction

Barcelona is the capital of **Catalonia**, Spain. It is located next to the Mediterranean Sea. Barcelona is a popular tourist attraction. People travel there to see its unique art and architecture. They visit Barcelona's beautiful beaches. Since 1899, local fans of soccer, known as football in Spain, have been waving their flags in support of one of the world's greatest professional soccer **clubs**.

Forward Luis Suárez has scored more than 100 goals since joining Barcelona in 2014.

Futbol Club Barcelona is one of the most supported soccer clubs in the world. It is known to fans as both Barcelona and as Barça. Barcelona is a symbol of Catalonia's culture. FC Barcelona is home to other sports, such as basketball and rugby, but the soccer team is the club's star. With record numbers of championships and well-known past and present players, Barcelona is truly a team to watch.

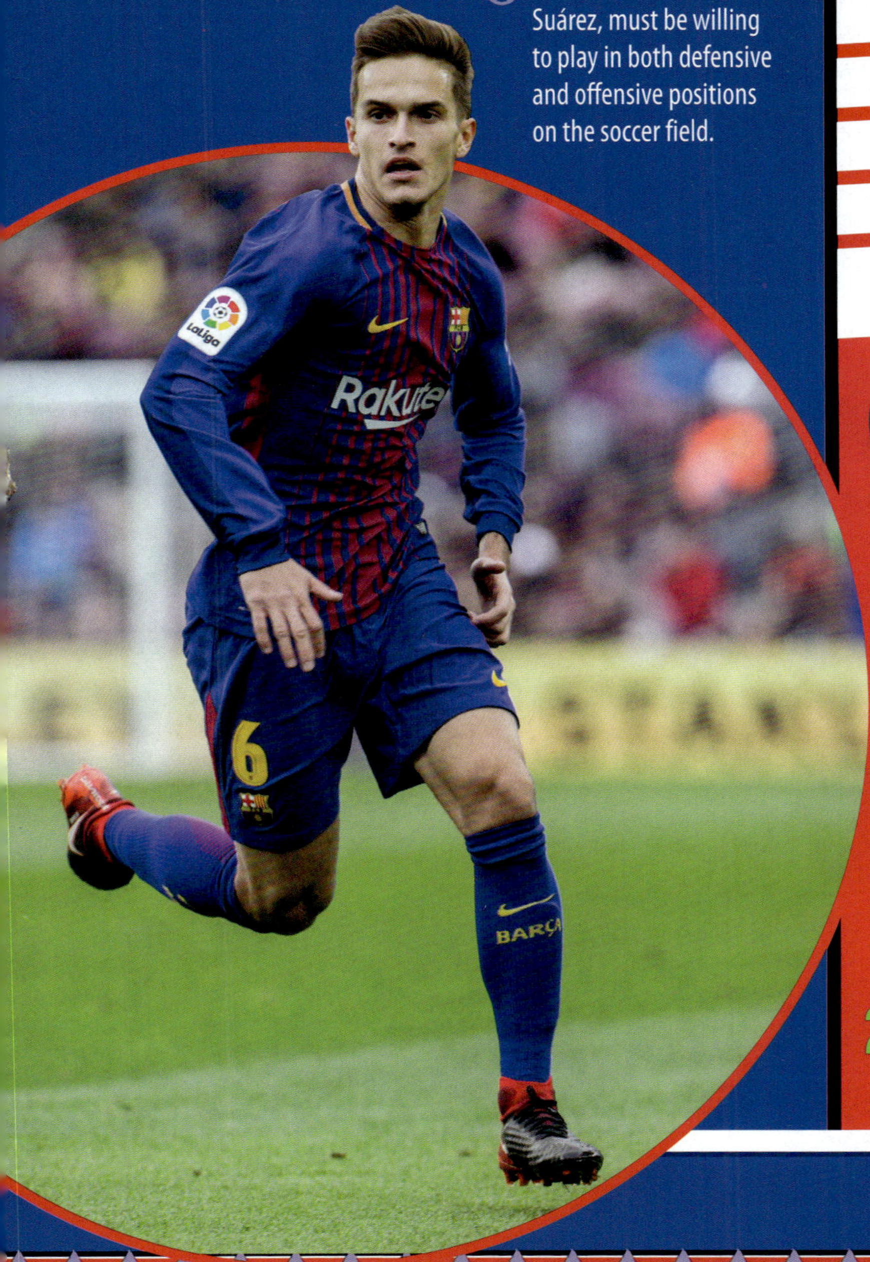

Midfielders, such as Denis Suárez, must be willing to play in both defensive and offensive positions on the soccer field.

FC BARCELONA

Arena Camp Nou

Division La Liga

Head Coach Ernesto Valverde

Location Barcelona, Spain

FIFA Club World Cups 3

Nicknames Barça, *Blaugrana* ("Blue and Reds")

67 National Titles

6 FIFA World Players of the Year

22 International trophies

20 Teams in La Liga

26.6 million Twitter followers

History

When Joan Gamper came to Barcelona for work, he placed an ad in *Los Deportes*, or "The Sports," Magazine, announcing his interest in forming a soccer team.

FC Barcelona was formed in 1899. It was an amateur team until 1910. The club's founder was Swiss businessman Hans "Joan" Gamper. Gamper also played for the team for several years, and served five terms as the club's president. He recruited club members to provide financial support. They helped the club build a new stadium. Gamper also hired Barcelona's first official coach. To this day, Barcelona is one of only a few member-owned clubs in Spain.

In the 1920s, Barcelona won many titles. However, Gamper's death in 1930 and the Spanish Civil War in 1936 made playing soccer difficult. Better times came in the 1950s. During the 1951–1952 season, Barcelona won five major titles with the help of **striker** Ladislao Kubala. The next three decades brought many changes in leadership and players. The club also built a new stadium.

Barcelona has won more than 60 titles and championships since 1983. A few Barcelona players returned as successful coaches in the 1990s and early 2000s. Some of the world's best players joined the team during the past three decades. Lionel Messi remains one of Barcelona's most successful players of all time. The team continues to find success with each new season.

Johan Cruyff played for Barcelona between 1973 and 1978. He then coached the team between 1988 and 1996.

The Arena

There is a chapel next to the players' tunnel going into the stadium. Players can stop on their way to the field and say a pre-game prayer.

Barcelona offers fans the "Camp Nou Experience," which includes access to the Barça Museum, the Messi Space, and a behind-the-scenes tour of the stadium.

Camp de les Corts, "Les Corts Field," was the first stadium built for FC Barcelona. However, after more than 30 years, they needed more space. The club started building Camp Nou in 1954. Barcelona played its first game at the new stadium in 1957. Camp Nou's seating capacity is just under 100,000. The stadium is the largest in Europe.

Camp Nou was originally named *Estadi del FC Barcelona*, "FC Barcelona Stadium." Fans referred to the stadium as *camp nou*, or "new field," and the name stuck. It is a traditional stadium with three seating tiers. Most of the seats are red and blue. A few yellow seats spell the words "FC BARCELONA" and the club's motto. The only covered seats are in the grandstand area behind the team's bench. Not much has changed at Camp Nou since it was built. For several years, the club debated about whether to build a new stadium or renovate Camp Nou. Barcelona decided to renovate the old stadium. Architects and builders will make it larger and more modern. The renovation will be finished in 2021.

After Camp Nou is renovated, it will seat 105,000. All the seats will be covered. The whole first level of seating will be rebuilt to make watching the games better for fans. Barcelona will continue to play in the stadium during the renovation process.

Even though it was renovated twice, Camp de les Corts could not hold all of Barcelona's fans and had to be replaced.

Where They Play

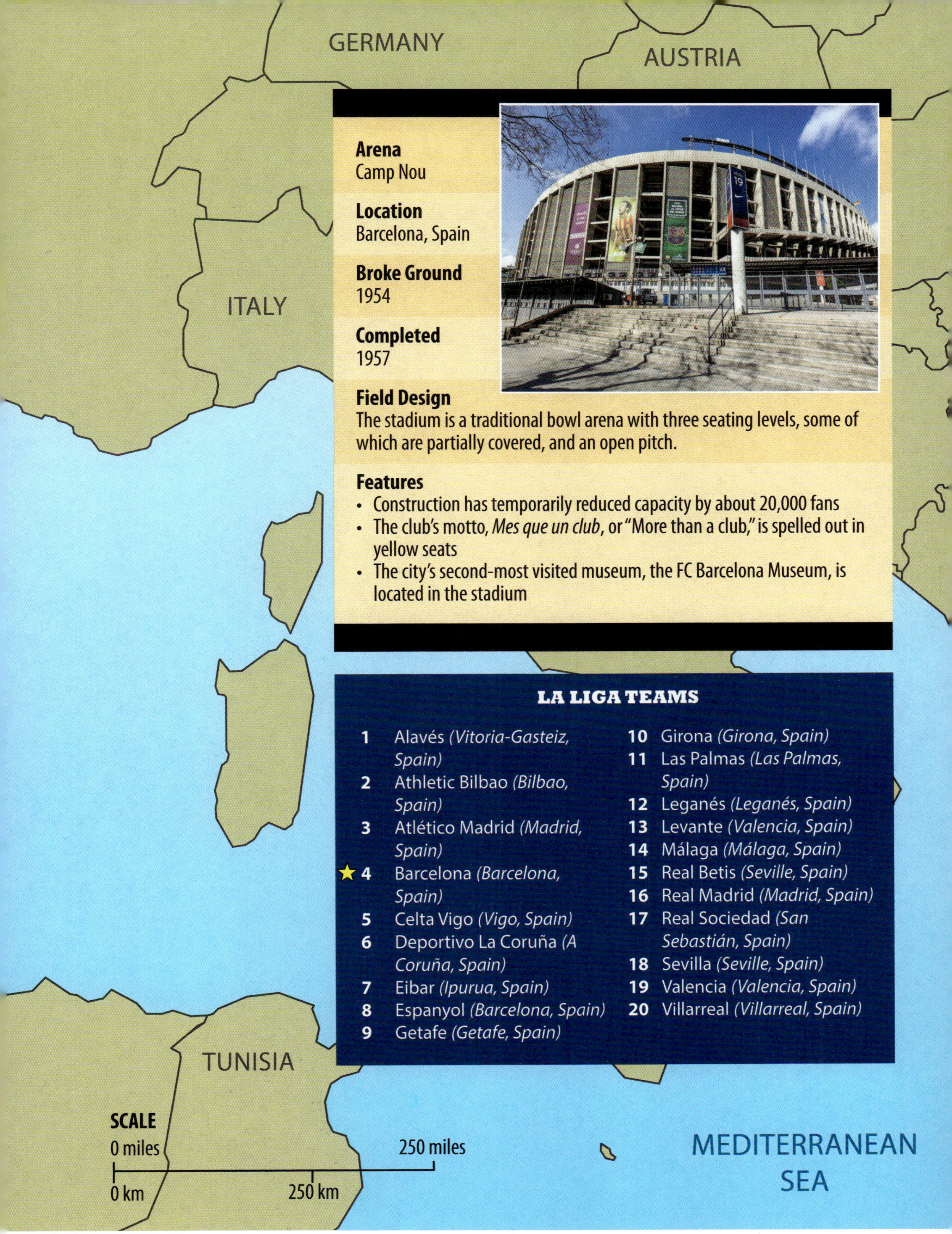

Arena
Camp Nou

Location
Barcelona, Spain

Broke Ground
1954

Completed
1957

Field Design
The stadium is a traditional bowl arena with three seating levels, some of which are partially covered, and an open pitch.

Features
- Construction has temporarily reduced capacity by about 20,000 fans
- The club's motto, *Mes que un club*, or "More than a club," is spelled out in yellow seats
- The city's second-most visited museum, the FC Barcelona Museum, is located in the stadium

LA LIGA TEAMS

1 Alavés *(Vitoria-Gasteiz, Spain)*
2 Athletic Bilbao *(Bilbao, Spain)*
3 Atlético Madrid *(Madrid, Spain)*
★ 4 Barcelona *(Barcelona, Spain)*
5 Celta Vigo *(Vigo, Spain)*
6 Deportivo La Coruña *(A Coruña, Spain)*
7 Eibar *(Ipurua, Spain)*
8 Espanyol *(Barcelona, Spain)*
9 Getafe *(Getafe, Spain)*
10 Girona *(Girona, Spain)*
11 Las Palmas *(Las Palmas, Spain)*
12 Leganés *(Leganés, Spain)*
13 Levante *(Valencia, Spain)*
14 Málaga *(Málaga, Spain)*
15 Real Betis *(Seville, Spain)*
16 Real Madrid *(Madrid, Spain)*
17 Real Sociedad *(San Sebastián, Spain)*
18 Sevilla *(Seville, Spain)*
19 Valencia *(Valencia, Spain)*
20 Villarreal *(Villarreal, Spain)*

The Uniforms

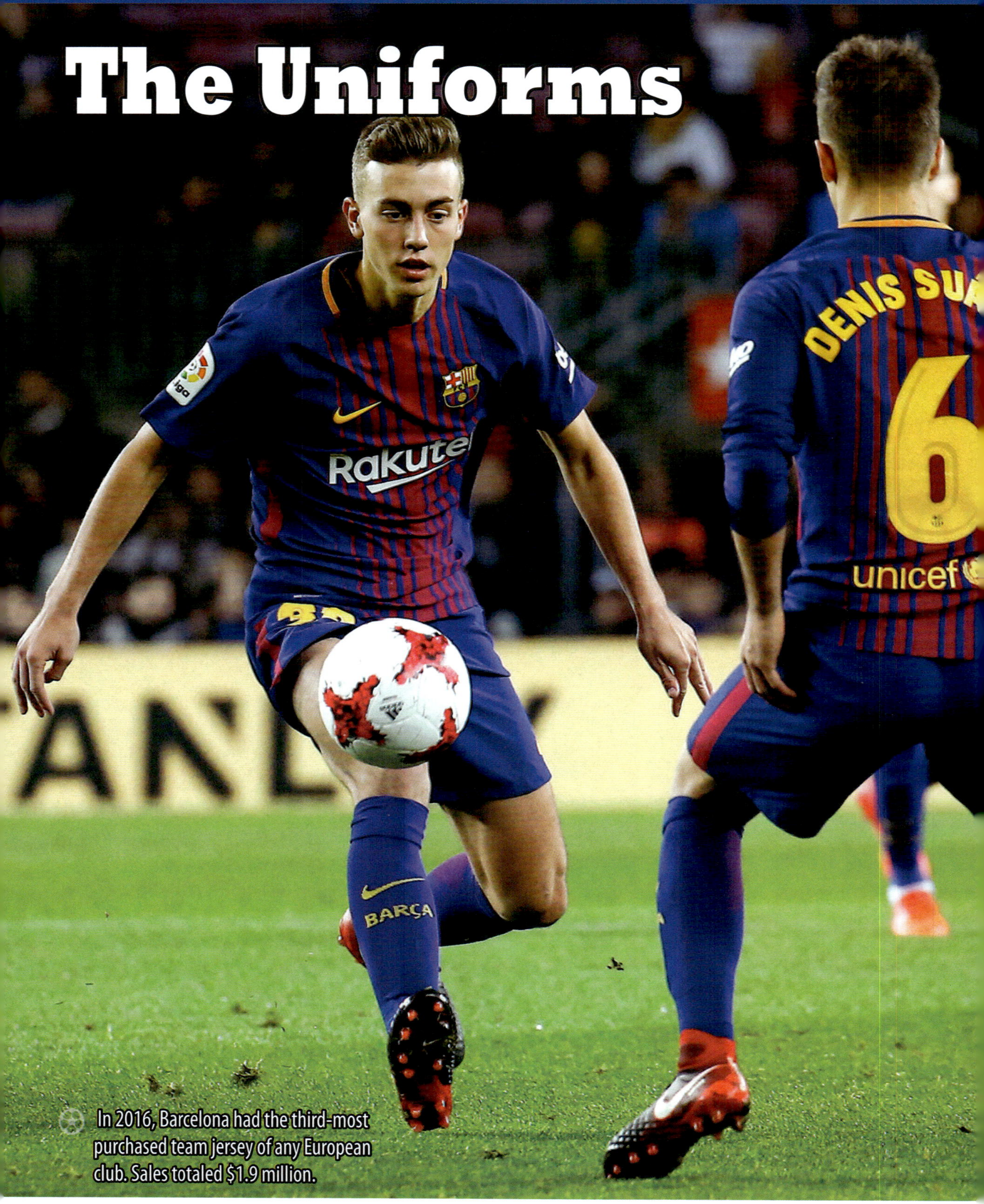

In 2016, Barcelona had the third-most purchased team jersey of any European club. Sales totaled $1.9 million.

Since the team's first season, every FC Barcelona home **kit** has featured blue-and-red jerseys. Players wore white shorts early on, but eventually those, too, were red or blue. The team colors are iconic. They even inspired one of the team's most common nicknames, the Blaugrana.

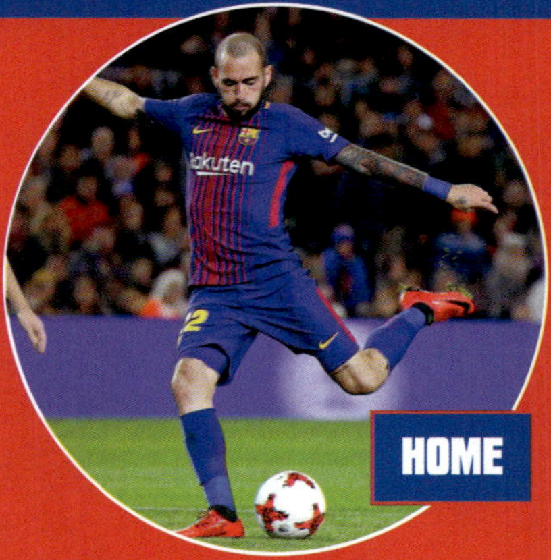

Barcelona's away kit varies greatly from year to year. It has been bright orange, dark green, and black. Barcelona sometimes wears yellow and red, the colors of the Catalonia flag, in away matches. As of 2017, the away kit is light blue.

The Barcelona logo has not changed much since 1910. The logo has the flags of Barcelona and Catalonia at the top. There are red and blue stripes at the bottom and a gold ball in the middle. A gold banner with the club's initials is in the center of the logo.

Before Barcelona had an official sponsor, the team partnered with the United Nations Children's Fund (UNICEF). The club continues to donate more than $1 million per year to the organization.

Goalie Gear

Marc-André ter Stegen is known for one-on-one challenges, often leaving the goal to stop a ball before the opposing player has a chance to shoot.

Goalkeepers must stand out from field players and field officials. Goalies usually wear long sleeves and often choose brightly colored jerseys. Keepers for Barcelona often wear bright green, red or black jerseys. They can wear pants if they choose. Most wear special goalkeeping gloves. These gloves have rubbery surfaces to help them grip the ball. Some goalkeeper gloves contain plastic spines to protect keepers' hands from injuries.

Barcelona's current top goalkeeper is Marc-André ter Stegen. He is the goalie for the German National Team. Ter Stegen replaced legendary Barça keeper Víctor Valdés in 2014. Fans had very high expectations of ter Stegen. Today, he is considered one of the best goalkeepers in Barcelona's team history. Ter Stegen often plays a **sweeper-keeper** role. He averages 33 passes per game, meaning he passes to teammates on the field rather than just punting the ball down the field.

Some goalies wear padded shorts or pants because of how frequently they dive for the ball.

The Coaches

Current Barcelona coach Ernesto Valverde's nickname is *Txingurri*, or "the Ant," because he is short and is dedicated to hard work.

Barcelona has had more than 50 coaches since the club was formed. The team's first long term coach was Jack Greenwell. Barcelona's current coach is Ernesto Valverde. He played for Barcelona and managed other La Liga teams before becoming head coach in 2017. He follows a long line of legendary Barcelona coaches.

LUIS ENRIQUE Luis Enrique spent only three years as coach at Barcelona. However, in that brief time, he became one of the club's most successful coaches. The team won 42 out of its first 50 games with him as coach. Enrique led Barça to the FIFA Club World Cup in 2015. Under his leadership, Barcelona earned 9 of 13 possible trophies.

PEP GUARDIOLA Pep Guardiola was the team's coach from 2008 to 2012. When Guardiola became coach, he replaced several players. He also changed the way the team played on the field. Guardiola stressed discipline and more defensive pressure. His leadership resulted in 14 trophies in 4 seasons. He is Barcelona's most successful coach of all time.

JOHAN CRUYFF Johan Cruyff was one of Barcelona's best-loved coaches. His "Dream Team" led Barça to its first ever European title in 1992. Cruyff is best known for starting La Masia, Barcelona's youth academy. He also implemented the **tiki-taka** technique at Barcelona. Lionel Messi and other Barcelona players still use this technique today.

Fans Around the World

Barcelona's average fan attendance for each game is 77,944. They have the highest attendance rate of any club in Spain and the second highest in La Liga.

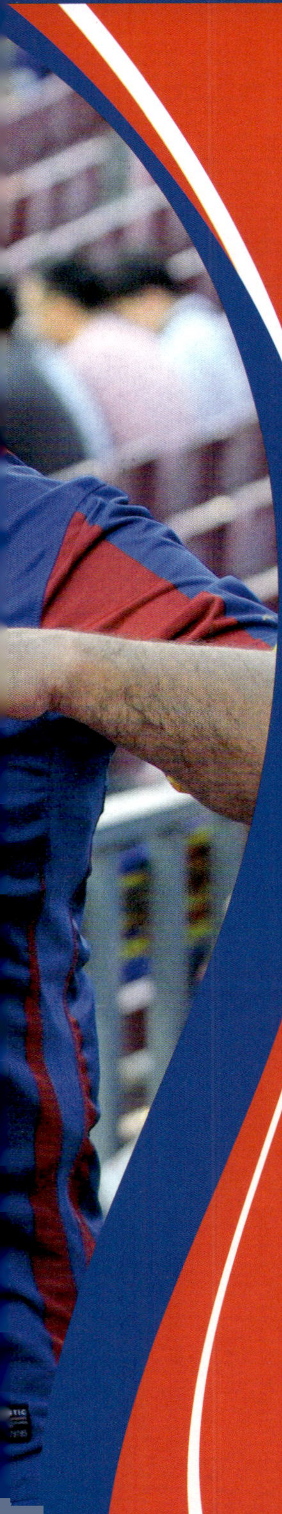

FC Barcelona is one of only a few fan-owned soccer clubs in the world. Some fans, called *socis*, meaning "members," pay a yearly fee to FC Barcelona. In return, *socis* get to vote for the club's executive offices. They also have a say in club issues and get extra privileges, such as discounts. *Socis* have special seating at all FC Barcelona matches.

There are more than 300,000 official Barça fan club members. There are FC Barcelona fan clubs in every country around the world. Each club is officially approved by FC Barcelona. Club members are called *penyes*, meaning "rocks" or "foundation." *Penyes* do not vote or have a voice in club matters. However, they receive discounts and special seating at matches.

Fan Traditions

#1 Pope John Paul II was an honorary member of FC Barcelona. He performed a mass at Camp Nou in 1982.

#2 Fans use colored flags and scarves to create **mosaics**, usually words and phrases, in the stands during matches.

Legends of the Past

Many great players have suited up for FC Barcelona. A few of them have become icons of the team and the city it represents.

Ladislao Kubala

Ladislao Kubala helped Barcelona become a winning team after many difficult seasons. His skill on the pitch was like nothing Barça fans had ever seen. Kubala was the first player to ever curve a shot. Fans filled Les Corts to see him in action. During his first full season with Barcelona, the team won every trophy and title possible. Kubala scored 280 goals for Barcelona in 345 matches. A statue of him stands on the grounds at Camp Nou. Kubala is considered one of the club's top players of all time.

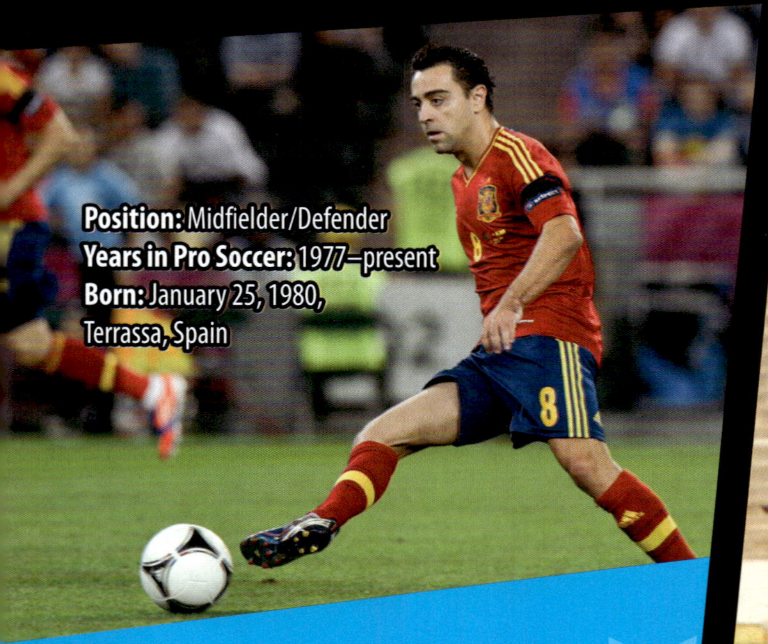

Position: Midfielder/Defender
Years in Pro Soccer: 1977–present
Born: January 25, 1980, Terrassa, Spain

Position: Forward/Striker
Years in Pro Soccer: 1944–1967
Born: June 10, 1927, Budapest, Hungary

Xavi

Xavier Hernández is known simply as Xavi. He began playing as a **defender** for FC Barcelona's Under 12 team as a child. Xavi eventually moved into a midfield position. He went on to score 84 goals for Barça. Xavi is able to find spaces to receive and pass the ball. This helped him create scoring opportunities for himself and his teammates. Xavi's mastery of the tiki-taka style of play made him a dynamic, dangerous player. He is considered one of the greatest midfielders ever to play soccer. Xavi holds the record for the most appearances for FC Barcelona.

Víctor Valdés

Víctor Valdés is considered one of Barcelona's all-time best goalkeepers. The team earned 26 titles, including two FIFA Club World Cups, while he was goalie. Valdés made 602 appearances with Barcelona. He set a team record during the 2011–2012 season by going 896 minutes without allowing a goal. Valdés won the trophy for the best goalkeeping record in La Liga five times. He was also a goalkeeper for the Spanish National Team until 2014.

Position: Goalkeeper
Years in Pro Soccer: 2000–2017
Born: January 14, 1982, L'Hospitalet, Spain

Johan Cruyff

Twenty years before Johan Cruyff managed Barcelona, he was a player for the club. Cruyff is considered one of the greatest soccer players of all time. As a player, he led the team to its first La Liga title in 14 years. Cruyff's unique style of play changed the way FC Barcelona played soccer. His style was called "Total Football." It involved moving into open spaces on the field rather than staying in a single position. Cruyff's approach to soccer continues to inspire players today. He was known in Barcelona as *El Salvador*, or "The Savior."

Position: Forward/Midfielder
Years in Pro Soccer: 1964–1984
Born: April 25, 1947, Amsterdam, Netherlands

Stars of Today

Today's FC Barcelona team is made up of many young, talented players who have proven that they are among the best in the league.

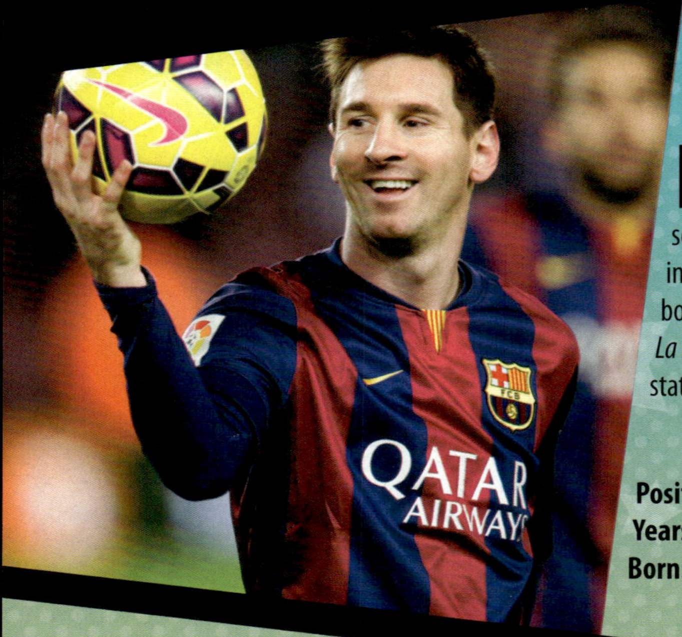

Lionel Messi

Lionel Messi is one of the best-known players ever trained at La Masia. He is widely considered the best soccer player in the world, with 30 team trophies and many individual awards. Messi is the all-time leading goal scorer for both Barcelona and Argentina's National Team. His nickname is *La Pulga Atómica*, or "The Atomic Flea." This is due to his small stature and his ability to change directions quickly.

Position: Forward
Years in Pro Soccer: 2003–present
Born: June 24, 1987, Rosario, Argentina

Andrés Iniesta

Andrés Iniesta has been the captain of FC Barcelona since 2015. Iniesta came to La Masia at age 12. He has made more than 600 appearances with FC Barcelona. Iniesta is known for being able to play many different positions. He is considered a playmaker who sets up scoring opportunities for teammates. Iniesta is also a starting member of the Spanish National Team. In 2017, he signed a rare lifetime contract with FC Barcelona. This contract ties him to the club for the remainder of his career.

Position: Midfielder
Years in Pro Soccer: 2001–present
Born: February 2, 1987, Barcelona, Spain

Sergio Busquets

Sergio Busquets is a master at reading the field and knowing where he needs to be. Busquets is one of FC Barcelona's top players. He is good at playing anywhere in the midfield. Busquets is also skilled at disrupting offensive attacks. He worked his way up to a starting role after joining the team in 2008. Busquets continues to impress with his passing skills, aerial attacks, and ball possession. He is the third captain for Barça, and has earned 25 titles with the team.

Position: Midfielder
Years in Pro Soccer: 2007–present
Born: July 16, 1988, Sabadell, Spain

Gerard Piqué

Gerard Piqué is a key defender for FC Barcelona. He is well known for attacking the ball in the air. Piqué usually plays center back, but is skilled in multiple defensive positions. Even though he is a defender, Piqué has scored 36 goals in his 10 seasons with Barça. He was part of FC Barcelona's Champion's League–winning teams in 2009, 2011, and 2015. Piqué is also a member of the Spanish National team, with 94 appearances and 5 goals.

Position: Defender
Years in Pro Soccer: 2004–present
Born: February 2, 1987, Barcelona, Spain

All-Time Records

3
FIFA World Cups
FC Barcelona has won the FIFA Club World Cup a total of three times.

6
Titles in a Year
In 2009, Barcelona won a record six official titles: the Spanish Cup, La Liga, UEFA Champions League, Spanish Super Cup, UEFA Super Cup, and FIFA Club World Cup

526
Goals Scored
Lionel Messi has scored 526 goals for Barcelona, and played in 608 games.

124

Official Titles

With 124 official titles, Barcelona is the most successful soccer club in Spain.

2

Trebles

Barcelona has earned two **trebles**, in 2009 and 2015, winning La Liga, the Spanish Cup, and the UEFA Champions League both years.

Timeline

Throughout the team's history, FC Barcelona has had many memorable events that have become defining moments for the team and its fans.

1909
With the help of club dues, FC Barcelona moves into its first home stadium, Camp de la Indústria.

1929
FC Barcelona and other Spanish teams form La Liga, which will become Spain's premier soccer division. Barça wins the very first La Liga title.

1890 1900 1910 1920 1930 1940 1950

In 1910, the club held a contest to redesign the team's official badge. It has changed very little since.

1922
Now a successful club with a membership of 10,000, FC Barcelona requires more space and constructs Les Cortes, the team's home stadium for the next 35 years.

1952
Ladislao Kubala leads Barça into a period of great success, winning five trophies in the 1951–1952 season alone.

The Future
In the past decade, FC Barcelona has achieved some of the greatest successes in the club's history. A combination of talented young players and familiar faces on the pitch hold much potential for the club's future. It is not difficult to imagine a future Barça team maintaining a place at the top of La Liga.

1957
Camp Nou, "the new field," opens to more than 90,000 spectators.

2004
La Masia alum Lionel Messi becomes part of FC Barcelona's first team. He goes on to become one of the greatest players the club has ever seen.

1960 1970 1980 1990 2000 2010 2020

1973
Barça signs Johan Cruyff, who is instrumental in bringing the club back to a period of many victories.

2015
Barça wins the FIFA Club World Cup for the third time. This is the team's 20th international title.

In 2017, FC Barcelona begins a massive renovation of Camp Nou.

Write a Biography

Life Story

A person's life story can be the subject of a book. This kind of book is called a biography. Biographies often describe the lives of people who have achieved great success. These people may be alive today, or they may have lived many years ago. Reading a biography can help you learn more about a great person.

Get the Facts

Use this book, and research in the library and on the internet, to find out more about your favorite player. Learn as much about him as you can. What position does he play? What are his statistics in important categories? Has he set any records? Also, be sure to write down key events in the person's life. What was his childhood like? What has he accomplished off the field? Is there anything else that makes this person special or unusual?

Use the Concept Web

A concept web is a useful research tool. Read the questions in the concept web on the following page. Answer the questions in your notebook. Your answers will help you write a biography.

Concept Web

Write a Biography

Adulthood
- Where does this individual currently reside?
- Does he or she have a family?

Your Opinion
- What did you learn from the books you read in your research?
- Would you suggest these books to others?
- Was anything missing from these books?

Childhood
- Where and when was this person born?
- Describe his or her parents, siblings, and friends.
- Did this person grow up in unusual circumstances?

Accomplishments off the Field
- What is this person's life's work?
- Has he or she received awards or recognition for accomplishments?
- How have this person's accomplishments served others?

Help and Obstacles
- Did this individual have a positive attitude?
- Did he or she receive help from others?
- Did this person have a mentor?
- Did this person face any hardships?
- If so, how were the hardships overcome?

Accomplishments on the Field
- What records does this person hold?
- What key games and plays have defined his career?
- What are his stats in categories important to his position?

Work and Preparation
- What was this person's education?
- What was his or her work experience?
- How does this person work?
- What is the process he or she uses?

Trivia Time

Take this quiz to test your knowledge of FC Barcelona. The answers are printed upside down under each question.

1 How many times has FC Barcelona won the FIFA Club World Cup?

A. Three

2 Who is FC Barcelona's top goal scorer of all time?

A. Lionel Messi

3 What is the name of FC Barcelona's youth academy?

A. La Masia

4 Which FC Barcelona fans pay for membership and are allowed to vote on club matters?

A. Socis

5 What famous religious figure was an honorary member of FC Barcelona?

A. Pope John Paul II

6 What year was Camp Nou completed?

A. 1957

7 What is the meaning of FC Barcelona's motto, *Mes que un club*?

A. "More than a club"

8 The FC Barcelona logo features red and yellow stripes in honor of which flag?

A. Catalonia

9 How many trophies did Pep Guardiola win during his time as FC Barcelona's coach?

A. 14

Key Words

Catalonia: one of 17 regions of Spain with its own language and identity. The city of Barcelona is its capital.

clubs: athletic teams or organizations

defender: also called a back. A player who plays in front of the goal and stops the other team from scoring.

goalkeepers: also called goalies. The players responsible for keeping the ball from going into the goal and the only players who are allowed to pick up the ball.

kit: the standard attire and equipment worn by soccer players, including a shirt, shorts, socks, and shin guards

mosaics: the use of colored cards, flags, or scarves by fans to create a word or symbol in the stands at a sporting event

striker: a forward player who is the team's primary scorer

sweeper-keeper: a goalkeeper who often leaves the penalty box to play the ball

tiki-taka: a style of play involving very accurate short passes and an emphasis on keeping possession of the ball

trebles: having won three major trophies in a single sports season or calendar year

Index

Log on to www.av2books.com

AV² by Weigl brings you media enhanced books that support active learning. Go to www.av2books.com, and enter the special code found on page 2 of this book. You will gain access to enriched and enhanced content that supplements and complements this book. Content includes video, audio, weblinks, quizzes, a slide show, and activities.

AV² Online Navigation

Audio
Listen to sections o
the book read alou

Book Pages
AV² pages directly correspond to pages in the book.

Video
Watch informative video clips.

Embedded Weblinks
Gain additional information for research.

Key Words
Study vocabulary, and complete a matching word activity.

Try This!
Complete activities and hands-on experiments.

Quizzes
Test your knowledge.

Slide Show
View images and captions, and prepare a presentation.

AV² was built to bridge the gap between print and digital. We encourage you to tell us what you like and what you want to see in the future.

Sign up to be an AV² Ambassador at www.av2books.com/ambassador.

Due to the dynamic nature of the Internet, some of the URLs and activities provided as part of AV² by Weigl may have changed or ceased to exist. AV² by Weigl accepts no responsibility for any such changes. All media enhanced books are regularly monitored to update addresses and sites in a timely manner. Contact AV² by Weigl at 1-866-649-3445 or av2books@weigl.com with any questions, comments, or feedback.